made for weather

made for weather

poems by

Kay McKenzie Cooke

OTAGO

Published by Otago University Press
PO Box 56/Level 1, 398 Cumberland Street
Dunedin, New Zealand
Fax: 64 3 479 8385. Email: university.press@stonebow.otago.ac.nz
First published 2007

ISBN 978 1 877372 49 0
Cover illustration: *made for weather*, Mike Cooke, 2007
Printed in Hong Kong through Condor Production
Published with the assistance of Creative New Zealand

creative nz
Arts Council of New Zealand *Toi Aotearoa*

poems

Southland

Taut, this road
we tear down – as tight
as steel-rope

strummed by speed. We feel
its hum under us
as it runs it beats

a tattoo under our thighs.
Over the Waiau, Aparima,
Oreti. Before Browns

we pull into a gate
where lambs mew and rock
to the bleat of mothers

calling out with voices
like humans.
At our backs now a spine

of mountains:
the Takitimus
caught and puckered

shoulder-to-shoulder
like brothers gathered
for a family snap,

on each head
the same blond shock
of snow.

earliest memory

My mother pushes the pram through
a forest of broom
to more solid, roadside shingle.

Had she taken a shortcut
and got us lost? Remembering back
yields my only clues: how tall

my mother was, how breathless
with laughter and how soft
the broom, as soft as the empty fingers

of gloves, the flowers as yellow
as near suns, their perfume as elusive
as the smell of moths.

rough craft

When my father ploughed
the ground would roll over,
expose its underbelly
of broken forests.

Behind the Massey Ferguson
the plough's burrowing blade
peeled back grass.
Uncovered gnarled ebony

of ancient wood and white,
finger-bone handles of cups.
Sometimes he'd bring home
wood, damp, black,

animal-shaped, its rough craft
perfect for showing how art
can just turn up.
When my father ploughed

the tractor *hrrrmmd*
like a snare drum as bagpipe gulls
clamoured for worms
above the earth's slit throat.

her steering wasn't the same

When Mum got her driver's license,
we were scared. Her steering
wasn't the same as Dad's.
She might go over the edge

of a gully with us in the car.
Then we got used to it.
Used to seeing after school
on particularly wet days

the small, grey Austin A40
with its easy-wipe, tartan interior
parked on a slight lean
where the gravel road sloped

towards the ditch.
It was easier for Mum too. She could decide
suddenly to go into Invercargill
for the day and drive down

to the school with our lunches,
knocking on the classroom door.
One day the teacher, Mrs Tarama,
asked me to open the door

and at the unexpected sight of Mum
standing smiling in her good, brown coat,
I shut the door again,
right in her face.

two sugars

Below double-bass
powerlines,
seasons are broadcast

in the rattle of bleached timothy
and flirt of russet.
A ladybird's apple-seed armour

is a bright tick on a stalk.
Not too far away,
in the house as it drifts

into afternoon tea, my father
plants under the table
his bootless feet,

docile, dog-eared
in woollen farm socks.
And from this long-grass bower,

this fragrant, earthy
withdrawal into a warm day's
blood-heat

of boredom,
I hear the high, skylark-clink,
the rapid chirrup

of metal-struck china
as he stirs two sugars
into black tea.

no new broom

In 1957 she didn't trust
'new-fangleds'. The brand-new electrolux
with its attachments lay still
in its box, its flexi-hose the neck
of a dead goose.

She far preferred
old brooms to any new
ones. Especially her favourite
with its bristles all leaning to the left
towards the ocean, worn down from years
        of sweeping.

evidence

In her eighties when she died
I found no grief evident
in my father's face, his hands
solid and square as garden forks spread
unwavering over the coal range
for the warmth to infiltrate
from fingertip to heart.
His love for his mother then just a fact
not able to be proved.
Like Good Friday's sky

remaining its 3.00 p.m. blue
or grey, not the black I expected
of God's old blood
and despite what Father Casey said,
nothing either in the shallow cave
in the clay bank down by the culvert.
        No stone rolled away,

no angels bright among the gorse
and on the day after the funeral,
my father back driving the tractor
and whistling through his teeth.

feast

For days a charcoal line
scribbled across the sky, marked the return
of thousands of sooty shearwaters;
muttonbirds; titi.

Weeks later in our wash-house,
a new kerosene tin packed
with their plucked, headless bodies
salted and flattened.

Then on our plates, a feast
of golden skin and underneath,
dark plum meat, the run of fat
down our chins.

We'd eat them with milky mashed spuds
and swede, the salty gather
at the corners of our mouths
a sting that was almost a rash

as we sucked the light fan of bones
for every last bit of juice and tendril.
After a day's boiling, draining,
boiling, draining and boiling again,

the whole house was soaked in the smell
of ceremony and aftermath.
Walls and curtains steeped in an essence
of ocean and smoke, salt and fire.

Rowena

When she came to play,
Rowena would bring red lipstick
so we could pretend
we were grown-ups. After she left,
Dad would say,
'You're too young
to be playing those games',
and look worried and a little lost, like
when he turned down the radio
so that we couldn't hear
Marty Robbins
singing 'Devil Woman'.

broadcast

My sister's melodica
is a small piano held to her lips.

My ukelele smells of warmed varnish
and slides easily out of tune.

We all sit in a horseshoe-shape
and play along to the classroom's wireless

broadcasting songs
like 'The Streets of Larado'.

In my head a picture forms
of a pale and dead cowboy

wrapped up in bandages
while outside thousands

of thistledown silently tumble,
each seed a star

rolling in on its cartwheel
of fine, silver hair.

Tom Dooley tree

There was an apple tree
we named Tom Dooley
and we'd sing to it

Hang down your head Tom Dooley,
hang down your head and cry.

Its bark felt like skin, with a little give.

The apples were large
cookers, red smudged into yellow,
        each with its own grub
that, when our teeth broke
the apple's flesh and let in light,
would fall to its knees,
        beg for its life.

wild mint and cutty grass

In the gully
we see the impaled skeleton of a cat

spread-eagled in a thorny bush
and recognise it
as our pet that had died in the summer,

its body tossed by our father
into blackberry autumn has undressed

to reveal its bones and grimace
surfacing
from under threadbare fur.

When I tell my sister the fragrant green
under our feet is wild mint, she cries.

She is afraid of mint that might growl
or suddenly leap. But it is the cutty grass,
its neat accuracy,

we must be wary of. And
this sluggish bog, reluctant to help,

that sucks and slurps at our gumboots
as, overhead, an unseen skylark
wrestles with the sky.

Bluecliff

Snake bites on the tideline, the clue
to shovel liquid sand until our fingers

divine the bi-valve that confirms: *toheroa*!
Then a wave's freezing biff knocks us

and grabs us under our armpits.
But we'll have it if we only keep our grip

and in the lull scrabble farther, twist
and pull. Then with a bucket full of shells

with pearly tongues protruding, our quota's reached.
Miserable with ear-ache and the chafe

of weighty, woollen sleeves, now we want only
to be rocked away over sandhills

inside the warm Vauxhall Velox, our elbows
still fizzing from the shock of the sea's cold brunt.

cutting across

In winter, when the air began
to darken
and freeze

and the five o'clock deadline
set by my mother
was reached, it was time

to cut back home
across waterlogged paddocks
so wet they whistled

like overseas broadcasts
full of static.
        Or in summer,

over paddocks too-quiet,
dry and booby-trapped
with spring-loaded hares

that if spooked
would explode
out from under my feet,

a bullet of buff
cutting trajectories dead ahead,
stalks sheered and torn asunder

with the sudden rip
and crash
of shattered grass.

trepidation

Remember
that inevitable trudge home
alone? Between daylight
and darkness, dusk, and how eerie
the blackbird's
confident outburst?

That panicky click of dags
from scattering sheep,
the nervous geography
of hills behind
and a wavering coast
before. Foveaux Strait

lying as flat as a paddock,
a scraping subject
spread at your feet.
Yet your fear
meant you never did
take the queenly advantage

for in the sunset, remember
how the sea was all cunning
winks and knowing
just how far you still had to go
before it would finally
drop from view?

gumboots bongo-drumming

My cousin had straight, fine hair that fell like black water.
When she moved away it was to a house in Papatotara

with a mailbox and a cattlestop at the bottom of a concrete
    driveway
and on the front lawn, a goldfish pond. When I stayed there we
    made plans

to get up early the next morning to gather mushrooms,
our gumboots bongo-drumming hushed paddocks

scented with sheep dung, pine needles and ragwort
as we roam a roomy world to pluck baby-pink tiddlers

still buttoned-up, or larger ones, unfurled, silky
and garnished with shavings of dirt. And even older ones,

with a tall leg and a mottled, browning table-top
already beginning to crêpe, the sooty pleats underneath bitten

and crawling with mites. We plan to go as far as the banks of the
    Waiau,
gaze at its rippling, liquid sinews, then head back to the house

with bumping bucket and my uncle's instructions a hiss in our
    brains:
to shut every gate we go through and whatever we do, don't go
    anywhere near

that grave-shaped gape near the electric fence – the offal pit – the
    dead-sheep hole
a trough we're just able to detect among grass bent double with dew

over where starlings crackle from knots of grey trees, hazy as a dream,
that cavity filled with carcasses and the throb, the dark hum, of
    pale maggots.

they thought

They thought she should have a boyfriend and suggested Dave
from the garage who took her for long drives at night
through tanned and treeless country and insisted on kissing
in laybys which only made her feel as lonely
as the moon looked. And when summer returned she left

that town of hit-and-miss kindnesses from people
who never admitted they knew all along her secret:
that she grieved for the baby she'd given away and how
she too listened to the wind at night that, if it could,
would hurl away all the hills and turn them to dust.

cigarette smoke in the rain

We were together two months: May,
June '73. He was funny, could be
tender, boyish, but felt the misfit

of islands, culture, climate; and his eyes
after drinking became bloodshot pokers,
his guitar-picking hands, hard fists

to fling a kitten against a wall, bash
taxi drivers, me. Even now, just the smell
of cigarette smoke in the rain is enough

to jolt me back to that bus-ride one wet day
out to St Clair beach for him to find some familiarity
in the sea's lap. As always, people looking at us

as we got on the bus, this Maori boy from Auckland
with the Southland blonde. He hated it,
the surf's cold spittle, its frosty haze.

And even as he said he loved me, hated
my advantages of freckled skin, of place,
of peace. He wore a light-blue, woollen hat

pulled hard down, jeans tucked tight
into rugby socks and black, laced-up bovver boots.
We caught the next bus back. Hardly said a word.

thaw

Already,
the sun's torched the snow. Powder
-puff powerlines are back to black,

thin lines. Noise returns to roads. Shrubs disrobe.
Trees unveil. The clear, white roof breaks
out into its usual bright rash. And lying

on our deflated lawn, a piece of coal
where a hawk-eyed sun has picked out
the snowman's eye.

what is important

Far out breakers rage
          – quiet eruptions

sudden as the flower
of an avalanche;

white and quick
as in darkness

and light alike
the ocean breeds wave

after wave. My heart too,
a sturdy carriage

of belief, beats
and waits for what

          after death splits the seed.

hemispheres

Fetid with winter's dead leaves,
the soil, as it warms
in spring, elbows out of its bed
the split seed. Birds beat
levered wings
and return to melted dams.
Grey gardens open eyes of violet.

It is our hemisphere's turn
now to tilt closer to the sun and it is glad
to rid itself of its glum winter coat, flash
its inner lining of kingfisher blues
and announce: Drinks of glassy sun
for everyone.
Oh and look! Ducklings

like brass coathooks
and following their mother's every move
as if on a string, until the pale eye
of a black-backed gull narrows
to pluck with excavator claws the infant
away. Someone somewhere shivers,
sleeveless in baby-soft sun.

Lee Bay, Stewart Island

The bay where my ancestors
Jacka and Timu lived, is where I want to go.
Lee offers me her car,
a beige Mirage, but real and gutsy

enough to get me there as long
as it gets plenty of choke. She says,
just take it, the keys are in the ignition
where they're always kept.

It's the Stewart Island way.
Before I go they tell me it's farther
than you think. That I can't miss it
it's right at the end of the road. But if I arrive

at a gravel pit, I've gone too far.
I follow a caramel road barged at
by bush. And there it is, a fingernail
-shaped bay, small, pale with sand and waves

that arrive wearing a chainmail of mist.
Boulders, sun-warmed, offer therapy
for the back like a taxi driver's beaded seat-cover.
I lie back, shut my eyes, smell rank,

rotting seaweed and try to sense kinship,
blood. Familiarity. To picture Timu here,
like the woman I see gathering kelp
a hundred yards away whose small child,

even farther back, wails at some drama
that has swallowed her entire world.
The mother continues to gather, bleats back
to the child, cold-comfort words.

go back to Gore

In the Gardens under bare trees
as dark as cracks, I heard a woman
I didn't know yell at two silent men.
'Go back to Gore where you all roll your rs
like Americans.' And turning on her heel,
she snarled, 'Gor-r-re'. All the way into town
as I walked, it tumbled in my mind
like a taunt; something personal.

cd

Heading for Gore and already
under a lofty, Balclutha sky.
        We stop for petrol,
on us the languid eye
of the uninterested
service-station attendant
as we pick through
the thin collection
of cds marked down, the covers
cloudy from being shuffled.
I recognise the hair,
its latin flip, the smile,
the sidelong tip, the slurred
look. 'Dean Martin!' I scoff. 'Dean Martin?'
said the BP man brightening,
'He was good when he used to jump up on top of the piano.'

old gum

Under my feet, neglected ground
and a sly rustle
from the dry litter of fallen leaves
curled like ploughs.

On my fingers, the vapour of gum-nut
to bring back memories of the swing,
its blanched, felted rope.
After breaking in the land,

this tree is the only thing
that remains of a time more robust,
when my grandfather's family of ten
were all still alive, playing rounders

in the house paddock. Of smoke seeping
from the ruined mounds of felled trees.
Of the time they dynamited a stump
stuck fast in mud.

Planted near his home as a reminder
for him of Tasmania, today this old gum,
with its severed limbs, even in the rain
still smells of sun and horses.

made for weather

I

Airy, lofty, leggy
eucalyptus,
has architecture

more modern
than classic. In the wind
it dances, shakes

out a fragrant, bouffant
hairdo. Like a house built
for harbour views

with glass and white,
plain space, it has designer-gaps
to see the sky through.

II

Whereas when hard-pressed
to ride the wind
and rain,

the pine
slugs it out. Stocky,
hairy, a dark and close beast

of burden
made for bad weather
with branches

shaped like arms prepared
to carry. Stuck for shelter,
I'd head for the pine.

shadowed veins

I watch as the mountains
become bearded with shadows

and a wind on all fours
        scatters the lake before it.

*

After death there is some small solace,
a measure

of comfort found in a pinch of memory.
Like the memory I hold of you,

your amused eyes
under a brow I thought was permanent.

*

In the grain of this wooden table,
a tree's shadowed veins

reminds me that time does not
discriminate

but in the end will always turn
wood to stone.

*

Through rain the falling scales
of a grey warbler's song

forms its familiar, mournful weave
of monotony and grief. Yet listen again

and it is the song of a bird
no bigger than an egg cup.

*

cold chariot

It's there,
        between pylons
and car-yards.

Set so far back
it's an entire world
that fits

inside my eye.
        I see it in full –
its silent traverse,

        its swimmer's disdain
for traction,
its wall-eyed advance,

this wild onyx moon
riding-up.

passing

The morning has opened up
just a little wider,
making the asphalt appear
beautiful and the sounds
from the school playground
echo like empty sky.

I pass three children holding hands, two girls
and in the middle, a freckled boy
with glasses and a two-day-old scar a ruby
chip on his nose, who looks up at me, says,
'Good morning'.
('Eager to please' written all over
his school reports.)

Holding his hand, his older sister
emits a tuneless hum.

giant grass

In dirt as warm as down
two boys build a fort from broken bamboo.

Plastic soldiers, navy-frigate blue
and moulded into frozen attitudes of war,

squint to aim needle-guns at giant grass
and the outer-space of blue

eucalyptus. Sometimes in their sights,
the cursive curl and loop

of blackbirds
across the afternoon's hard light.

They plot onslaughts,
declare the wisdom of camouflage

and plunder the ground for rough twigs
of dead pine and leaves of dock.

And the closeness of dancing birds
calms and fixes my heart

as if forever on the lazy harbour,
the milky ocean,

as these soldiers safely wage
their strange and immobile war.

crosscultural

My soup, brown and warm, arrives
in a plate as heavy as a skillet.
'Ha, ha, ha, ha, ha,' guffaws a mallard.
'You can't hurt me, I'm with my Dad,'
a little boy shouts from the playground.
'Do you guys celebrate Easter?'
the Irish waitress with a long, blonde plait
asks a table of four Asians.
When they say they don't she says,
'So, no chocolate Easter eggs then?'
unable to conceal her tone of woe.

strangely parted

To my children
I've always been old.
A tree, never the sapling.

A sunset
without the sunrise.
As far as they're concerned

my life began mid-stream
– a ford for them to cross
over in safety.

Like photos I've seen
of my own mother
taken before I was born,

when she was twenty-one
and a stranger wearing shoes
and a coat I'd never seen

before, her hair young,
springy, strangely parted
to the side. Girlish,

she's as thin as a parcel
still wrapped-up, smiling
an oddly unencumbered smile.

like a tree

Look at yourself
at fifty-one
in some changing-room

mirror. How generous
the double helpings
over the wiry frame

that used to be
more obvious.
How much there

now to seize
with both hands.
Like a tree,

the older the wider.
Look! How much
life has grown on you.

each verandah

Homesick for the more familiar
ocean and rain,
I was lost
in that inland town tied to willows
and a river,

where each strange verandah
painted bright, each snug window,
neat hedge,
suggested something more sinister
than the mere unwinding

of a fortnight's holiday
where the light was hot
and dark-liquid fly-traps
festered in five-gallon drums.
But the swimming hole –

reached over ground rough
with raspberry,
with its rope swing
and smell of mud –
gave off the smell of home

and for a time there,
I would revel
in the Waikaia's attentive rocking,
my limbs under water, wavering
pale and unfamiliar.

found

(for my daughter Ro)

I never knew you
except intimately; you were
my own, my flesh. Then
I never knew you at all

except in thought.
Or imagination. Or as a dream
as real as a fact.
Your imprint, as faint as a star

out there somewhere;
a face I'd lost and looked for
often, only assuming
it to be beautiful. And I was right:

when you found me
I found you
were still a heart beating
under my own heart.

after thirty-seven years

How you'd have hated it, being that weak ghost
I dream of, the insubstantial father

too self-centred and ill to engage.
You'd prefer to be a dead hero,

the Larado cowboy of your songs, cold
as clay and long lamented. And you have been.

Time now to address that dreamed imposter,
instruct it to remain under its weathered headstone,

or in its own paradise of green hill and stream
alone with its feeble heart and bloodless wounds.

For that pale invalid is not the real you.
You are ancestral-strong, beyond sight and sound, yet

not unwitnessed. You are the grin I hear in the corner
of my eye.

writing on a tree

In winter, trees retrench and rivers
wait for summer's adornment
of children at swimming holes
with near-drownings, a toe-hold
on gravel slipping out from under.
Like my brother who gasps for air

but takes in only water and then
the mad leap from my father, this
the second such timely rescue;
my cousin too, nearly drowning
in a lagoon if not for my father,
who when he died, did so alone

without witness or saviour
in the Otautau Catholic church's
toilet, six feet by six, that still stands
unnoted. These trees I see today
are deemed to have more worth,
and if cut down, men would weep.

Yet if that small, wooden building
was demolished, the only ones to mourn
would be his children, now middle-aged,
left behind by a father who never gave a thought
to the willows or poplars, or cabbage tree
down by the creek.

Once in a breezy plantation of pine
I selected a tree to scrape a heart
into the bark with a knife
taken from the cutlery drawer.
I wanted to know what it felt like
to write on a tree.

I remember the scent of sap
and the rough ground underneath,
earthly cold, a mouldy carpet of amber needles
that deadened footsteps, and the jagged light
beyond the trees, sharp on grass
paddocks as soft and round as bellies,

as bright and green as parrots
and where my father, yet to die,
twirled the tractor in casual figures of eight
as he topped thistles, silver-tipped
as a river trees grow beside
and winter just around the corner.

nothing to do with you

For a cup of coffee,
you would strike the heart

with an axe, mine stone
for its marrow.

Maim
what rolls on into sky. Screw

metal poles into quiet land,
warp and crush

its offer
of light and air.

*

For northern power,
on land nothing

to do with you,
you would trammel

quilted, southern ground, leave
a trail of stains,

thrust twisted crosses
into its soft belly.

*

Rocks the wind or sun
cannot move, sleep on.

Tussock-backed
they carry soft gold

sound
we can hear for miles.

From somewhere,
a farmer

calls his dogs. Somewhere,
the blaring throats

of young bulls
we cannot see.

Under our feet the gravel
coughs. Fallen apples

form a wild carpet
below a crooked tree.

*

The mist freezes
where it wafts, solid

lace. Cold, bloodless
and beautiful. Still for days

on end, the sun a smear
across the sky's white mouth.

Bulrushes stuck fast
in frozen ponds.

Willows and poplars
as wan as horse-hair.

*

In summer, the grasshopper
screams. In summer

the road floats
grey. Purple lupins

and orange poppies
dribble paint.

When we stop the car
we hear overhead

a pair of paradise ducks,
their alternating cries

the unfenced sound
of a mountain tarn.

*

Seized by the autumn sun,
valleys do not resist

the line and fall
of riverbeds and trees.

'We call this
our golden season.'

She speaks among art-deco
lightshades.

'Here, we don't get that fog
they get down river.'

And as the railway station's
useless clouded window

veils the sky's
cruel blue,

she talks of a small town now gone,
and the shop she ran for years.

*

On land nothing
to do with you, somewhere

the sound of a tiny bird.
Somewhere, lovely light,

the sound of nothing, of no one,
of the air.

near Alexandra

A western sky suggests
the promise of air loosely tethered
and space and light. Of breath
blowing through
the pleat of mountains.
Warm wind through wire.
Of opening out
        an accordion of sun.

'my little grasshopper plane cannot fly very high'*

We listen to music from records that smell of warm tar,
opening the windows wide to let the sound through.
And despite the dark-green pine
and the orange-tiled roof of the house
against the hill, there are darker things
to consider in these wobbling, afternoon hours:

an imminent death, how chancy our lives,
last night's dream. I tip my head right back
like a child drinking rain
and see at once how blue and terrible
a sky without clouds. How blank, like a mirror
that refuses to show me my face

and leaving me without the benefit of borders
or wings. You turn the record over
to play side two. I tell you about the dream
last night of my father, dead now
thirty-seven years and how I heard him
say, 'See how right you were to trust me?'

* *A line from the song 'Lost in Paradise' by Caetano Veloso, released by Sergio Mendes and Brasil '66 on the album* Stillness.

aftermath

It's the quiet after singing frogs have leapt
leaving behind the fizz of bubbles bursting
around a lily pad's leather fist.

Sometimes it's a longing
to crate the fully-grown frame of them
back into that solid container

now scattered – home's safe encasement:
the three of them still asleep in one room,

the wheat smell of warm, young hair
damp and malty
with the sweat and brew of dreams.

all that

The last to leave home, we'll miss
his unwashed frying pan
thick with the amber lace of fried egg,

the abandoned, empty shoes looking helpless
and far too big for any son of ours.
His choice of adjectives, 'wicked' and 'primo';

the verb 'gutted', the phrase 'pretty much sucks'.
The 4.00 a.m. Sunday-morning clank and creak
up the narrow hallway.

The toilet light left on all night, a blaring, lighthouse
globe to guide moths through the peril
of open louvres. Yes, we'll miss all that, plus

stretched out on the couch his crashed, sleeping body;
the tender snoring, his long, hairy legs
as sweet as baby pungas.

the Crown

Rattray Street has a certain
tattoo-parlour charm.
Streetlights sprout
from heaped tar stained with beer.
A broken skyline clambers
for morning's quick fix.

On the corner, the Crown,
and inside, one fiery heater
with hot, orange breath
to warm cold knees,
and on the toilet doors
nursery rhymes about drugs.

It is an old hotel with old walls
with frozen portraits
of bad, grey memories
painted over many times. Like mine
of that day standing there
outside the door

in the garter-stitch hat I wore
all through that winter,
knitted in the shape of a bell,
its multi-coloured wool the shade
of a bruise. Of a sky
bleeding blue.

map making

Tonight my sister-in-law Hilary phones
from Beaumont. She wants to know when
my mother's due down from Palmerston North
with cuttings for our gardens. I tell her
nothing specific as I can't find anything
on either calendar or map. She says I sound flat,
I say, 'No, just tired'. A statement designed
to give the impression of being noble;
someone the world relies on. The truth is
I have relocated to somewhere inside my head
where no one can find me, not even you
when you bring me a cup of coffee and two squares
of Turkish Delight, holding them out in front of you
as if to light your way to wherever it is you think I am.

piecing together

As large-faced dreams leave me,
I hear a bird's fearful joy.

The light, crushed by cloud
into dullness, shows the sky

never did intend to remain
faithful to its province of blue.

You search for a needle
and, when you find one,

hold its eye to the window
and thread it with caution.

It is only now with the light behind
that we learn to read more slowly.

Today we will head south
across plains where sheep the shape of bales

suckle at the water table,
to a levee-town built and steadied

by farmers with huge hands.
Where shelter belts fifty years old

have been axed at the knees.
Where the inevitable green

spreads flush with foothills.
Our love does not need speaking of.